Finding a Better Way

Finding a Better Way

Edited by
JEANNE C. DEFAZIO

Forewords by
MARTHA REYES and OLGA SOLER

Afterword by
FRANCOIS AUGUSTIN

WIPF & STOCK · Eugene, Oregon

FINDING A BETTER WAY

Copyright © 2021 Jeanne C. DeFazio. All rights reserved. Except for brief quotations in critical publications or reviews, no part of this book may be reproduced in any manner without prior written permission from the publisher. Write: Permissions, Wipf and Stock Publishers, 199 W. 8th Ave., Suite 3, Eugene, OR 97401.

Wipf & Stock
An Imprint of Wipf and Stock Publishers
199 W. 8th Ave., Suite 3
Eugene, OR 97401

www.wipfandstock.com

PAPERBACK ISBN: 978-1-6667-0502-7
HARDCOVER ISBN: 978-1-6667-0503-4
EBOOK ISBN: 978-1-6667-0504-1

07/22/21

This book is dedicated to those treated with less courtesy and respect and viewed as less intelligent or less trustworthy on the basis of race, color, sex, ethnic origin, age, and disabilities.

By the Same Authors

Francois W. Augustin

Christian Egalitarian Leadership: Empowering the Whole Church According to the Scriptures (contributing author)

Jeanne DeFazio

Creative Ways to Build Christian Community (ed. with John P. Lathrop)
How to Have an Attitude of Gratitude on the Night Shift (with Teresa Flowers)
Redeeming the Screens: Living Stories of Media "Ministers" Bringing the Message of Jesus Christ to the Entertainment Industry (ed. with William David Spencer)
Berkeley Street Theatre: How Improvisation and Street Theater Emerged as Christian Outreach to the Culture of the Time (editor)
Empowering English Language Learners: Successful Strategies of Christian Editors (ed. with William David Spencer)
Keeping the Dream Alive: A Reflection on the Art of Harriet Lorence Nesbitt (author and editor)
Specialist Fourth Class John Joseph DeFazio: Advocating for Disabled American Veterans (editor)
Christian Egalitarian Leadership: Empowering the Whole Church According to the Scriptures (contributing author)
An Artistic Tribute to Harriet Tubman (Ed. With Julia C. Davis)
The Commission: The God Who Calls Us to Be a Voice during a Pandemic, Wildfires, and Racial Violence (editor)

Martha Reyes

Keeping the Dream Alive: A Reflection on the Art of Harriet Lorence Nesbitt (contributing author)
Specialist Fourth Class John Joseph DeFazio: Advocating for Disabled American Veterans (contributing author)
Redeeming the Screens: Living Stories of Media "Ministers" Bringing the Message of Jesus Christ to the Entertainment Industry (contributing author)
Jesús y la Mujer Herida (Jesus and the Wounded Woman) (author)
Jesucristo, Tu Psicólogo Personal (Jesus Is Your Own Personal Psychologist) (author)
Por Que No Soy Feliz (Why Am I Not Happy?) (author)
Quiero Hijos Sanos (I Want Wholesome Children) (author)
The Commission: The God Who Calls Us to Be a Voice during a Pandemic, Wildfires, and Racial Violence (contributing author)

Olga Soler

Just Don't Marry One: Interracial Dating, Marriage, and Parenting (contributing author)

Tough Inspirations from the Weeping Prophet Apocalypse of Youth (author)

Creative Ways to Build Christian Community (contributing author)

Epistle to the Magdalenes (author and illustrator)

Redeeming the Screens: Living Stories of Media "Ministers" Bringing the Message of Jesus Christ to the Entertainment Industry (contributing author)

Berkeley Street Theatre: How Improvisation and Street Theater Emerged as Christian Outreach to the Culture of the Time (contributing author)

The First Book: Nature; The Second Book: Time Travel, Adventure, Romance, Faith; The Third Book: Revelation: Revelations Series (author)

Empowering English Language Learners: Successful Strategies of Christian Educators (contributing author)

Keeping the Dream Alive: A Reflection on the Art of Harriet Lorence Nesbitt (contributing author)

An Artistic Tribute to Harriet Tubman (contributing artist)

The Commission: The God Who Calls Us to Be a Voice during a Pandemic, Wildfires, and Racial Violence (contributing author)

Contents

Acknowledgments | xi
Foreword by Martha Reyes | xiii
Foreword by Olga Soler | xvii

Finding a Better Way by Jeanne DeFazio | 1

SECTION ONE | 5
Defining Strategies and Frameworks for Conversations about Racial Reconciliation | 5

SECTION TWO | 25
Diversity and Inclusion in the Interracial Family | 25

Afterword by Francois Augustin | 31
About the Authors | 35
Bibliography | 39

Acknowledgments

THANKS, WILMA FAYE MATHIS, for reading the manuscript and making helpful suggestions. Lynn Forester de Rothschild deserves mention for creating and implementing strategies to include the economically marginalized. Thanks to Caleb Loring III, who supported this work, my niece Ella Ryan, who stands for racial equity, and Mark Douglas for being a wonderful neighbor!! I am indebted to Peter Lynch for his kindness. I am especially grateful to all those I cannot name in this work. Most of all, I thank Jesus for giving me the strength to carry on.

Jeanne DeFazio

Foreword

Judging by Stereotypes

Martha Reyes

I was born in Puerto Rico, a small island in the Caribbean and a US territory. Even though Puerto Ricans are born US citizens, our primary language is Spanish, and the predominant cultural roots are more in tune with the rest of Latin America. Puerto Ricans are a masterful blend of light-skin Spaniards, Taino indigenous, Black, and mulatto (the olive-skin children of the Black and White that have been interbreeding throughout many generations). It is for that reason that skin color was never an issue for me. My friends in elementary and secondary school were diverse, almost a second family, with no notion of prejudice, discrimination or racial preference, or exclusion.

When my family moved to California back in 1972, the panorama changed. Way back then, it was not easy to find groups of Latinos, much less Puerto Ricans. One Latino student group in college was made up of about twenty members originally from seven different countries. (Now we are everywhere.) I decided to join them since I was more comfortable speaking my language sharing the cultural comfort zone. But something strange began to happen: Latinos were checking me out and sizing me up because I did not fit the profile of the stereotypical Latin American: even though I feel Hispanic to my core, I am White, blonde, blue-eyed, quiet, and I do not enjoy salsa music or Mexican food, or loud speaking at family reunions. "She is not one of us."

So, I decided to join other campus clubs, such as the university choir, the campus art club, the student union, etc. But, then again, I felt I did not belong there either. The large student population was Anglo, so the language and cultural differences were notorious. They often could not understand my heavy Spanish accent or my strict family-oriented moral and religious upbringing. In my home, there were rules for everything, and an absolute matriarchy operated my household. Many new friends would find that odd, a bit too much, so they would not consider me part of the inner circle, especially if mom wanted to chaperone all our gatherings.

My English got better and my intercultural skills too. I polished my musical skills and began to perform as a singer/songwriter at interesting venues while finishing my primary career in psychology. I studied hard in various colleges and universities in California and became a Doctor of Clinical Psychology. I was invited on many occasions to be a guest lecturer or public speaker. And now, a new group of critically analytical people analyzed me. Why? I would show up dressed as an artist, grabbing the microphone as a singer, and feeling everybody's eyes on my clothes, shoes, makeup, and stylish looks: no thick eyeglasses, no gray hair, not enough wrinkles for them. I did not look like your typical college professor, so they questioned my credibility and credentials.

It became evident to me that discrimination, intolerance, and exclusion manifest themselves with different shades, and they are not necessarily based on skin color. They seem to come more from preprogrammed assumptions, unrealistic expectations, and an unconscious habit of bundling groups of people into a prejudged status without allowing them to demonstrate themselves in their true gifts and virtues. Many missed opportunities for not enjoying or benefiting from other people's unique gifts; instead we sabotaged the moment with fear or rejection!

As a psychologist, I now understand that our primitive brains try to protect us from anything that is quickly perceived as an unknown or unfamiliar. When we first meet someone or when we walk into a situation for the first time, the initial reaction is excess of precaution to assess the level of trust or threat. Shortly after, we must resist the unfair critical judgment and thirst for more information with an enhanced sense of familiarity and even compassion. Because not only physical traits have gone through an evolutionary process; emotions such as fear, complacency, satisfaction, joy, and many others are also subject to transformation. For example, fear of the unknown could transform itself into rejection, resentment, discrimination, or prejudice. When we do not give ourselves the necessary experiences to neutralize or invalidate fear, we accidentally raise its value and authority over our thinking processes and will. Sociopolitical narratives also manipulate anxiety and other feelings in our hearts, convincing us that it is somehow understandable and acceptable to hate opposite views and opponents just as much as we have justified hating Nazis, Communists, slave owners, ISIS killers, and rapists.

Hatred is human devaluation, regardless of the team, the emblems, the flags, or the skin color. We need to take the time to talk to each other, neutralize inhibitions and fears, identify with honesty the good in all of us, analyze with insightfulness and empathy. Only then can we transition to peace, trust, appreciation, and love. Those who hate are engaged in psychological warfare, trespassing boundaries of dignity and spiritual identity.

Rejection and hatred will be conquered not necessarily when we find commonality, but when we learn to value and respect essential differences that exist to make us marvel at what others have and move us to incorporate those gifts into the canvas of human existence.

Foreword

The Magna Carta of Christian equality is stated in Galatians 3:28: "There is no longer Jew nor Greek, slave nor free, male nor female, because they are all one in Christ Jesus."[1]

---

1. Martha Reyes, interview by email, February 21, 2021.

Foreword

Fighting Profiling

OLGA SOLER

I HAVE HAD MANY instances of profiling in my life, even though, as an actress, my light-colored skin made me a flexible ethnic candidate for casting. I was invited to lunch by a friend when I was in Missouri and his stepfather would not eat at the same table with me because I was a *nigger*. I have been stopped by police at night who searched my car and person because of the braids I had in my hair when I was a mother of three and attending seminary. I have been insulted by police at the station where I was calmly advocating for the innocence of a friend. I have been warned to stay out of certain neighborhoods because of White supremacists in England and because *my kind* was not welcomed even though I was doing nothing against people's privacy or against the law.

Profiling is an evil we must all guard against and a book like this is very important, especially for those who claim to believe in the very ethnic Jew, Jesus Christ.

In the movie *42*, about Jackie Robinson with Chadwich Boseman in the leading role, we saw the struggle the first Black baseball player to play with the White major leagues had in being accepted. We see the enormous prejudice he faced and this in recent history. The way he won the crowds to his favor despite the fury of hate against him was to be a gentleman and to turn the cheek while playing the game like the champion he was. In the book *Where Do We Go from Here: Chaos or Community?*, by the Rev. Martin Luther King Jr., we see this dilemma on a mass scale, and here Dr. King makes his case for a peaceful demonstration showing how violence works against us.

When I counsel women who are trying to get their children back in a situation of domestic violence I often admonish them to check themselves. Make sure they have no addictions or violent habits of retaliation when they go to court. Nothing that the perpetrator's attorney can point a finger at because, at best, they will also be accused of addiction or violence and, at worst, a clever lawyer can turn things around and make all the problems in the home her fault. It is very much a war against spiritual evil we face when we come against profiling, abuse, and racism. If the enemy can find a reason to point the finger at us, we will lose. We will always lose.

I was a radical in my youth and was part of peaceful protest as well as militant protest accompanied by violence. I am convinced today, as a follower of Jesus, that we must fight evil with good. To fight evil with evil puts us in the camp of our enemies and we are not experts there. The Lord Jesus said we can only treat others the way we want to be treated. If we do anything else, then we deserve what we get. I would rather (God help me) go down righteously than with my hands stained with blood, even the blood of an abuser.

How do we fight profiling? This is how I think we can. Be everything they do not expect us to be. Be kind, intelligent, dignified, firm in what we are asking; become qualified, stand tall, and show them we are worth respecting. Learn to love the people God is making us. Respect ourselves. It is self-hatred that is the greatest hook racism or sexism has in us. Seek education so we can stand toe to toe with our accusers in a civil manner. Learn how to defend our view and our humanity with evidence. Not the nonsense on the Internet, but real books are the best sources here. I know education is a stacked deck because education for the poor and minorities is sorely lacking and getting worse all the time. Nevertheless, there are still libraries. We can educate ourselves. We can become informed. They say, *If you want to fool around, go to college; if you want to get an education, go to the library.* I wish every child and adult who wants to get a higher education was able to afford one in this country, like they can in other countries, but until that happens we can still learn enough to defend ourselves.

Immigrants or native Hispanics should learn English. You may love your mother tongue but you need to be able to know what they are saying. You also need to get resources that are available: grants, immigration lawyers, free counselors at community service agencies, etc. Don't stop moving either. In other words, decide you will move forward in your life every day. It is those who give up who lose. Make one inch of progress in your spiritual, emotional, and physical life daily, by the grace of God, and you will be miles ahead by the end of every year. As women in any field will tell you, we have to prove we are better than they think we are. It's not fair but it's a fact of life. This is a war against evil we are fighting and we have to get our game faces on. *Do all you do with all your might for the glory of God.*

Last but not least, don't profile. In his aforementioned book, Dr. King said we can't profile all those in the dominant culture. Some of them are on our side and it will be a coalition of them and us that will make the breakthrough with the help of God. We can't do it without them. We need to encourage them to step out with us and for us, as some of them feel prejudice is wrong but do not feel compelled to do anything about it. I once told a brother who was very supportive of women that he needed to speak to other brothers about the need to support women. He said he did not think he had the strength to do it. I told him I would pray for his courage. In retrospect, I should have told him I believed he could do it. We need to encourage each other to do good works and find friends for equality wherever we may. Then start and build a community to fight the chaos.

Foreword

In conclusion, the movie *42* had a scene where the owner of the Dodgers, Branch Rickey, played by Harrison Ford, was trying to console Jackie after he had walked off the field because the manager of another team had insulted him in the vilest manner before a huge audience of jeering spectators. Robinson was understandably at his limit of patience and in anger smashed his bat on the walls to the entrance of the field. Rickey, who was a Methodist and true believer, had hired Robinson because he was a good player but also because he was a Methodist and true believer. Robinson accused him of not knowing how he felt, to which Rickey replied,

> I don't know how you feel! You do! You're the one living the sermon. In the wilderness, forty days, all of it, only YOU! . . . We need you, everybody needs you. You're medicine Jack.[1]

As believers, we can talk about how Christ was rejected and how he suffered, but he said we would be treated the same way. Why? Because evil, with its subtle forms of profiling and prejudice, will never go down easily. There is a price to pay for being *medicine* in an evil world, or as Christ called us, *the salt of the Earth*. There will no doubt be victories but there will also be setbacks. Like Dr. King, we may go down fighting, but the fight will go on. King died but every day a child watches *Sesame Street*. The legacy of King goes on as this was a project of early education that Coretta King helped to sponsor after Dr. King's death. It's not a perfect show but it teaches kids to read and it shows that people of all colors are worthy of learning and can coexist peacefully together. Will we take the risk and walk tall into that arena? That is the question for us.[2]

---

1. Helgeland, *42* (screenplay), scene 132.
2. Olga Soler, interview by email, February 13, 2021.

Finding a Better Way

JEANNE DEFAZIO

Color blindness fundamentally misses the mark by erasing something that's fundamental to people's identity and people's self-love.[1]

WE ALL JUDGE OTHERS on appearance. In 2020, I became a distance learning teacher. Pre-COVID-19, I traveled from California to Massachusetts to teach. One early morning flight, I was standing in preboard and airport security came through and frisked a young Middle Eastern–looking man standing in front of me who spoke with a heavy accent. We had all gone through TSA (Transportation Security Administration) so it appeared to be an unusual concern. A well-meaning blond-haired elderly woman behind me alerted the airport security to the fact that I was carrying a travel bag onboard and looked Middle Eastern! She insisted that I should be checked also! I had been up all night and was very tired and started laughing. The airline attendant at the desk quickly let me onboard. At check-in, I had asked for more time to board. She apologized to me about the incident. I assured her that I was all for airport security but that I felt bad for the young man who got frisked. Nobody apologized to him. He was innocent but

---

1. Raël Nelson James, quoted in Vinipal, "5 Ways," lines 98–100.

phenotypically suspect. When I tell this story, it is to identify how easy it is to pass judgment based on ethnic stereotypes.

Every day as a child in the classroom, I put my hands over my heart and repeated:

> I pledge allegiance to the Flag of the United States of America, and to the Republic for which it stands, one Nation under God, indivisible, with liberty and justice for all.

I am grateful that this was a mandatory patriotic exercise in my youth. After George Floyd's death, the words came back to me to reinforce my faith in God and my country. During the 2020 breaking news reports of racial violence, I found comfort in Acts 17:26: "God hath made of one blood all nations of men to dwell on all the face of the earth." I recalled the words I love from the Declaration of Independence:

> all men are created equal and endowed by their Creator with certain inalienable rights that among these are life liberty and the pursuit of happiness.

My dad loved baseball. He played in a local league when I was a child. One of my favorite memories was going with him to get a baseball signed by Willie Mays. He sat in the back of a flatbed truck while a crowd stood around him silently. I called out "Say Hey Willie" and he smiled. I mention this because meeting Willie Mays impacted my childhood. I am grateful to have grown up believing that God blessed America and that all men were created equal, and during the time when Willie Mays played for the San Francisco Giants!

In April 1968, just before I graduated from St. Francis High School in Sacramento, California, Martin Luther King Jr. was assassinated. During that period of racial violence, I recited the words of a prayer attributed to St. Francis of Assisi:

> Lord, make me an instrument of your peace; where there is hatred, let me sow love; where there is injury, pardon; where there is discord, union; where there is doubt, faith;

where there is despair, hope; where there is darkness, light; and where there is sadness, joy.[2]

I believed that these were words St. Francis actually prayed. I loved the fact that my high school was named after one of the most venerated saints in Christendom. He raised the bar, letting us see the light of Jesus in a dark world. Because of the influence of my alma mater, I wanted to sow peace where there was hatred. During the 2020 racial violence, I got an email to attend a virtual Zoom meeting on racial reconciliation at St. Francis High School. Leaders in the faculty and community discussed strategies for racial reconciliation. That meeting gave me the idea for this book. As a teacher, I believe that we all learn best from each other.[3] I asked friends to describe an experience of being judged by physical appearance, the ability to speak the native language, or religious and cultural background. The end result is this wonderful collection of conversations from ethnically diverse contributors using the art form of writing[4] to promote inclusion and as an antidote to structural racism.

Brother Curtis Almquist, SSJE, explains:

> "Normal will never return, I hope not." An African American friend said this to me recently. She was speaking about the experience of injustice and suffering that has been so poignantly exposed during the coronavirus pandemic: the strains and inequities in healthcare, the economic disparity, the hijacking of hope and trust, the infectious cynicism, the display of racism. We have right

---

2. Scholars maintain that "Make Me an Instrument of Your Peace" is widely but erroneously attributed to Saint Francis. "Prayer of St. Francis of Assisi," *Wikipedia*, lines 17–24.

3. "Peer learning should be mutually beneficial and involve the sharing of knowledge, ideas, and experience between the participants. It can be described as a way of moving beyond independent to interdependent or mutual learning." Boud, "What Is Peer Learning," lines 7–9.

4. "The benefits of arts activities are being seen beyond traditional settings, and their role in supporting communities and individuals who would otherwise be excluded is increasingly being recognized." "Arts Health and Well Being."

now the opportunity to make changes in how we live and share life together. How shall we begin?[5]

---

5. Curtis Almquist, "Making Meaning," 10.

SECTION ONE

Defining Strategies and Frameworks for Conversations about Racial Reconciliation

Indira Palmatier

INDIRA TAKES A STAND for English language learners, facilitating conversations about "what's wrong" but also explaining "what could work." Indira created practical tools and a skill-based framework, which is important in conversations about diversity, equity, and inclusion.

> Growing up as an immigrant in England in the 1950s and early 1960s, I experienced the value ascribed to accents. As a child I remember a con- tinuous mild dread that came with feeling "one down" to the dominant society. One aspired to being as much like the "upper crust" as possible, with accents that, today, sound like speech impediments. If you had that accent the world opened up to you. If not, you could expect to be relegated to the lower echelons, your footsteps barely heard. Could there not be some vein of resentment at this pressure?
>
> So, the question is what to do with a possible, almost organic, resistance to the very idea of changing something so ingrained as a language with all its nuances and

nurturing. One could start right there. Questions such as "What are some important parts of your own language? What are things your mother said to you that you still remember? Please say these out loud in your mother tongue. How do you carry them with you? What do you feel when you hear your own language versus struggling to make yourself understood in another?" (powerless, stupid, disregarded, an irritation?). The longer the description the better—don't be afraid, just stay present, stay patient. The concept of "join and lead" begins to come alive. Besides the obvious, that it will help you get along in this society, how else might it be useful to learn English in a way you haven't thought of before? And, if that happened, then what else could happen? After that what else could open up for you personally? Who else could benefit? How? How would your identity change, who would you then be? Don't accept monosyllabic answers, express your faith that the students have the answers already within them. Eventually, with this line of reasoning one looks for "freedom" as the ultimate answer. And everyone wants freedom!

Important in goals to strive to reach is to listen as long and as deeply as one can. Only after all is "emptied out" is the receiver open to a new approach, a new possibility. At that point, when the goal is clear and bright, beautiful and beckoning, the teacher holds a precious hope for the future.[1]

Frances Kai-Hwa Wang's article "California Governor Signs Bill to Develop High School Ethnic Studies Curriculum" begs the question: can education legislation promote racial reconciliation?

> California Gov. Jerry Brown signed new legislation Tuesday to develop a model curriculum for ethnic studies in high schools, according to the Office of the Governor. Bill AB-2016, was sponsored by Assemblymember Luis A. Alejo (D-Salinas) and had bipartisan support in both houses. "AB-2016 is a landmark law that will ensure all California high school students have an opportunity to

---

1. Indira Palmatier, interview by email, May 23, 2017, quoted in DeFazio and Spencer, *Empowering English Language Learners*, 90.

Defining Strategies and Frameworks

> learn about their own or another culture's history and importance in shaping the state's past, present, and future," founder of grassroots education news and civic tech site K-12 News Network Cynthia Liu told NBC News. "We hope mutual understanding, empathy, and racial/cultural literacy will be the fruit of this important law. The law requires the California Instructional Quality Commission to develop—and California's State Board of Education to adopt—a model curriculum in ethnic studies, according to Alejo's office. This curriculum will be developed with ethnic studies faculty from California universities and public school teachers with experience teaching ethnic studies.[2]

Educators need to create the space to talk about race. While student teaching in a California public middle school, I gave a life skills lesson to a class after an adolescent male student tore the burka off the head of a female African American Muslim student during class. I was required to send him to the vice-principal's office immediately. Eventually, the mother of the female student took legal action. During the remainder of the class, I engaged the students in an exercise that reenacted the incident as an interactive instant replay. The students identified and modeled appropriate behavior. The group participation kept the students focused and enhanced their understanding as they participated in real dialogue around the issues of racial and religious justice. They took from that class the hands-on experience of upholding equal rights too often entrenched in racial disparities.

> The death of George Floyd and the protests that have followed sparked a national dialogue about race in America. For many, discussions about race and the reality of living in America as a black person happen daily. But many households, communities, and workplaces are having these conversations for the first time. How can employers and colleagues better support employees of

---

2. Wang, "California Governor Signs Bill," lines 1–14.

color? What is the most productive way to talk about race in the workplace?[3]

Charlie Lehman

Lehman's reflection on "Christians and American Racism" is an excellent framework preparing readers for constructive conversations about race and equity.

> Over the past couple of decades, conservative Christians have stood up and sacrificed for endangered human life, *specifically* fetal life. Now conservative Christians oppose others who stand up and sacrifice for endangered human life, *specifically* Black life. Conservative Christians point to the violence, law-breaking, hypocrisy, and stated opposition to the institution of the family they have detected in the Black Lives Matter movement. I dispute the moral high ground of a movement characterized by assassination, intimidation, law-breaking, and hypocrisy. Where was the conservative Christian outrage at the death of half a million Iraqi children whose parents, unlike the parents of American unborn children, struggled in vain to keep them alive?
>
> Who questions the values expressed in our founding documents? But, as the character Jackie Cogan points out in *Killing Them Softly*, the movie based on George V. Higgins's *Cogan's Trade*, the man who enshrined the inalienable rights of men kept his son in slavery. The expressed values are routinely superseded by the *other*, dark values. Some pro-lifers and Black Lives Matter activists make sacrifices for the victims of these other values, *specific* human beings.
>
> My mom followed Christ better than I do. She worshipped, helped to found a church in her old age, visited the sick and elderly, cared for her mother and aunt in their final days, and put up with me. But, as I remember it, she accepted Emancipation as America's answer to racism. If she were aware of the statutory racism of

---

3. Raël Nelson James, quoted in Vinopal, "5 Ways," lines 1–8.

Defining Strategies and Frameworks

restrictive covenants and their damage to Black families, I don't remember her speaking about it. I don't believe my mom understood that the woes of Black Americans in the twentieth century were *not* their own fault, that official and corporate America put them where they were and kept them there for the benefit of White America.

I do not know how current these figures are, but I wouldn't be surprised if the only differences would be reflected in their sources—FBI? The Innocence Project? As I understand it, non-Whites are treated more harshly at each stage of the criminal procedure: pretrial, trial, sentencing, and appeal. A lawyer complained to me and his officemate about an LSD sales case he'd been assigned—the only thing his client had going for her was her white skin.

My first assignment at the Los Angeles County Public Defender was felony arraignments. I got so used to the horde of low-level Black and Hispanic clients in the grungy, packed lock-up behind the courtroom that I was taken aback by seeing an institutionalized Japanese-American convict there on a new case. *His* presence there was not *normal*. As a paralegal, I benefited from the examples, kindness, and mentoring of Black, Hispanic, Asian, and White superiors and peers for twenty-five years. It was like Carl Weathers's respect and kindness shown to a young, tense actor.[4]

Jozy Pollock

As a former chaplain to the Los Angeles County Jail, Jozy ministered to the incarcerated from every race. While many professionals feel ill-equipped on what to do when it comes to diversity and inclusion, Jozy Pollock built a safe space and practiced engagement.

Jozy recently reflected on the multicultural community she developed as a chaplain ministering alongside Mel at the Los Angeles County Jail. She commented that, while watching a recent Christian television program, she was

4. Charlie Lehman, interview by email, February 17, 2021.

shocked to hear a white pastor say that if a Latino or African American attends his church he redirects them to a church of their ethnicity where they would be more comfortable. In her own words: "He wasn't even wearing a hood." Jozy's main ministry as chaplain focused on the incarcerated in the Los Angeles County Jail, which is multicultural but has fewer whites. Racism was rampant in the jail. God moved her to write a sermon on racism, which she preached to the inmates. She was surprised when God told her to take the same sermon to the church. She was on the pastoral staff at a church called The Hiding Place (a multicultural church filled with "the beautiful people" in the entertainment industry), and she preached her sermon when the pastor was away. Out of obedience, after Jozy preached the sermon, she shocked herself by inviting people who were racist to come forward for prayer. People did come forward and received prayer. During Jozy's decades ministering at the jail, she explains that she got along with all the gangs except the white supremacists, who one day explained to her that heaven was "all white." She replied: "No, it isn't." One white supremacist exclaimed: "Well, if it's not, I don't want to go there." Jozy responded: "Don't worry. You won't be going there." Currently, she happily attends a multicultural church with a tattooed ex-gang-banger pastor who, prior to conversion, was shot five times and stabbed three times.[5]

This pastor was converted in a facility where Jozy preached the Word.[6]

In her endorsement of *An Artistic Tribute to Harriet Tubman*, Jozy explains:

> Harriet Tubman was a powerful bold Black woman who risked her life at a time when it was believed by some that Black people didn't have souls. We have come far since then but still not far enough.[7]

---

5. Spencer and Spencer, *Christian Egalitarian Leadership*, 120.

6. DeFazio and Spencer, *Redeeming the Screens*, 69.

7. Jozy Pollock, Davis and DeFazio, *An Artistic Tribute to Harriet Tubman*, back cover.

Defining Strategies and Frameworks

Wilma Faye Mathis

My experiences have made me realize that it is important for managers to empower employees and provide them with resources for having productive conversations about race. I am sharing my experiences of racial discrimination in the workplace to stand up for African American women. I believe that every person should be treated as a human being and not better or worse depending on the color of their skin. I am voicing my experience of discrimination to bring healing into my own life and into the lives of those who read this book. I believe in the Scriptures, which do not promote racism, but boldly state: "There is neither Jew nor Gentile, neither slave nor free, nor is there male and female, for you are all one in Christ Jesus" (Galatians 3:28).

Today, Black women work in a variety of jobs and industries at all different levels. Yet Black women still confront the same misperceptions about their work that have formed at the intersection of racial and gender biases for decades. As a result, Black women face unfair expectations, unique challenges, and biased assumptions about where they fit in the workplace that differ from the perceptions held about women from other racial and ethnic groups as well as men.[8]

As a project specialist, meetings were part of my job description for updates, project status, and next steps. It was exciting to be at this level and invited to attend meetings with other managers. My manager at the time attended some of the meetings. He was always critical and found something to disagree with me about, but he was never wrong. I was called into his office to discuss my presentation. His first words were, "You present well, but would do better by stating the facts as I told you" and I agreed to do as suggested. Still in the same posture, he said, "I've been here a long while. You're pretty cute, and there can be a future for you here." By this time I am angry, not only with his posture, but with

---

8. Frye, "Racism and Sexism," lines 71–76.

his subtle advances and how I was being looked upon. I dismissed myself from his office, giving him the "look," and said, "My presentation will have what you suggested the next time" and walked out. My first instinct said to go to human resources, but I felt there was not enough proof to justify what I encountered. Did I also mention this manager had clout, talked loudly, abruptly, and was intimidating to people? I knew from here on it would be uneasy passing him in the hallways. One day, while he was with one of his male counterparts and passing me, he said, "Black but pretty." I was a naïve young lady at the time, but, looking back now, women's inequality existed then, just as it does today. It had been common knowledge this manager was powerful, and rarely confronted, but he was also involved in illegal matters that finally caught up with him. This resulted in him being no longer employed at this corporation. It is my hope that speaking the truth of my experience will root out and eliminate future gender and sexual harassment, which is a manifestation of structural racism.[9]

Aaron "Ezra" Mann

I met Aaron over thirty years ago in Los Angeles and am honored to be his friend. I caught up with him recently in Palm Desert, California, where he currently lives. He's a brilliant playwright who gained recognition in the film industry as an Academy Award–winning producer. His sense of humor is self-deprecating and always makes me laugh. Humor is a healthy way of processing as an ethnic stereotypical persona of an oppressed yet phenomenally successful minority.

> German-born American producer, writer, and director Aaron "Ezra" Mann is most probably best known for co-producing *In the Region of Ice*. This motion picture won an Academy Award (Oscar) for the best short live-action drama of 1977.

---

9. Wilma Faye Mathis, interview by email, February 1, 2021.

Defining Strategies and Frameworks

With the birth name of Icek Jakob Fiszmann, Aaron's life has been enriched with a theatrical family legacy spanning well over a century! His aunt Dora Zlotnik was a popular Polish silent-film screen actress. Her career started when she was cast as an extra in Charlie Chaplin one-reelers. Miss Dora (stage name) toured across Europe's most beloved opera houses and cabarets, performing live her unique Vaudevillian style of song and dance. Fortunately, Aaron's parents did survive the war (in spite of stints in German internment camps). His mother, Jean, was born in the small town of Sosnoweicz. Her father, Ruben Zlotnik (Aaron's grandfather), was an Orthodox Jewish rabbi from the highly regarded family the Zlotnik rabbinical dynasty. Ironically, this particular area of Poland was also home to the future who's who of Hollywood, such as Louis B. Mayer, Harry and Jack Warner (Warner Bros), Myron Selznik, Adolf Zucker, Paul Muni, Pola Negri, and Schmuel Gelbfisz (later changed his name to Samuel Goldwyn). Aaron's father, Samuel, was also born in Poland in the larger city of Lodz, which is the birthplace of Roman Polanski. The nearby city of Warsaw was home to Film Polski, where Roman attended. At that time, Film Polski was considered by many to be the world's finest film school.

After the war, Aaron's father apprenticed as a projectionist/cutter for Central Filmen Productions in Munich, Germany. Central specialized in the making of company training, military, and institutional films. Samuel later became one of Germany's most sought-after theatrical film producers.

Interesting side note: In the 1970s, while Aaron was attending the American Film Institute, he was most fortunate to have Slavko Vorkapitch as a professor. The professor formerly taught at Film Polski and it was him that introduced the famed Swedish director Ingmar Bergman to Aaron while visiting the campus.

"MOVE YOUR F***ING CAR, YOU DIRTY JEW!" Anti-Semitism, persecution, racial slurring, etc. One must not take these accusations seriously. Why? Because the name-caller doesn't *personally* know you; he or she merely knows an array of derogatory slang terms that pop out of his or her mouth with not much thought. Furthermore, I would say these perpetrators are less enlightened and caught up in their own negative world (easy to do) and haven't tapped into their "spine." By spine, I'm referring to our God-given anchor that's been installed into each and every one of us at birth. How do we tap in? It's a process that has several basic elements. For starters, forgive others. Bless them. And thank the Lord for revealing his wisdom. You will feel better and well equipped for the next time. Turn something negative into a positive![10]

Louise Maguire

Louise Maguire has worked with culturally diverse, criminally insane, and juvenile delinquents as a psychiatric social worker. Her clinical skills and empathy has won her awards and high regard.

> I was employed as a clinician in a juvenile detention center providing direct services, including individual and group psychotherapy as well as case management services. The majority of my clients were Hispanics who entered this country from Central America. They were primarily monolingual and spoke Spanish only. The majority of my clients escaped in search of reunifying with family members. There were others who traveled through Mexico trafficking drugs for the cartels. Most clients were of low socioeconomic status. The majority were held on felony crimes such as murder, aggravated assault, sexual assault, and burglary; therefore, the majority of these clients were ineligible for amnesty. The clients were males between the ages of eleven and seventeen. The majority were later incarcerated by the Department of Juvenile Justice and incarcerated in jail at eighteen years of age. I never interfaced with family members to witness any family reunification. Unfortunately, I was also totally unsuccessful with finding any family members, despite numerous inquiries. The majority of these youth seldom

---

10. Aaron Ezra Mann, interview by email, February 8, 2021.

Defining Strategies and Frameworks

expressed remorse for their alleged criminal behavior. I observed numerous assaults by these youth on both staff and peers. This detention facility was frequently on lockdown due to episodes of violent behavior. There were no incidents of these youth being transferred to community-based placements; these youth were then sent to the Department of Corrections upon discharge to either await trial or serve sentences. It is very sad to state that their future outcomes were rather bleak despite their very tender ages.

I developed trust by providing empathy, rapport, and positive, strength-based communication. I expressed social disapproval of all inappropriate behaviors, especially racial slurs. I promoted appropriate behavior with individual counseling to encourage assertive communication and provided very strong verbal praise. I practiced modeling appropriate behavior without engaging in either physical conflicts and/or making verbal threats. I encouraged practicing alternate coping skills with strength-based strategies. I verbalized the very vital importance that both following the rules and following their individualized service plans would result in a possible transition to a community-based placement. I constantly encouraged the clients to follow their service plans to graduate to a lower level of care. I encouraged the youth to use their words to verbalize their anger without engaging in physical conflict. I provided both ethnic and favorite foods of choice, such as tacos, papusas, fried chicken chips, and salsa, Takis, potato chips, cupcakes, and cookies. I celebrated both holidays and birthdays with hands-on activities and food. I consistently acknowledged both the educational and vocational opportunities that are abundant in this very wonderful country. I would encourage them to follow rules and study hard to take advantage of these opportunities. I repeated the following: "Please follow the rules of this facility." "We follow rules and ensure success." "There are also infinite opportunities awaiting you." "By modeling appropriate behavior and following the house rules, you will be able to transition to a community-based facility." "Following the rules also assures graduation of this transition successfully." I had a wonderful Christian supervisor and I was allowed to share my faith when appropriate. My prayer life skyrocketed while working with these clients. At the onset, the clients treated me with contempt and hostility; at the end of the term of my service, they thanked me for caring and food incentives. In spite of the grim realities of their life circumstances, we bonded as clinician and clients in a positive way.[11]

Julia C. Davis

Much of the undercurrent of annoyance and fury surrounding the recent killings of black men in the media are not just about the killings, but how it is rooted in a build-up of injustices felt in every corner of society.[12]

In her testimony, Julia Davis acknowledges the injustices present and is committed to resolving them by initiating productive and respectful conversations. What is amazing in this account is the way that Julia engaged the police force, gaining their support, empathy, and compassion.

I have experienced both overt and covert racial prejudice in my lifetime. I am sharing this experience as an African American because I see the potential in it to bridge the racial divide.[13]

In the midst of the pandemic and shortly after the onset of the racial violence following the death of George Floyd, my husband and I traveled from Massachusetts to California. We got a call from a California hospital regarding my husband's only and elder sister. She needed our help. COVID-19, violent protests, and heightened dissatisfaction with the status quo were backdrops to travel to bring her from the West Coast to the East Coast. With determined resolve, my husband and I became intrepid travelers and overcomers on our return with his sister,

---

11. Louise Maguire, interview by text, February 7, 2021.
12. Truitt, "Race Relations in the Workplace," lines 101–3.
13. Julia C. Davis, interview by email, 2/1/21.

Defining Strategies and Frameworks

who needed twenty-four-hour care. I never anticipated riveting Fourth of July memories such as materialized during this year of fear. We were actually confronted by four police cars, two of which were unmarked, at the airport shuttle terminal. God's favor, mercy, and grace were profoundly prevalent in what could have easily escalated into a dangerous, life-threatening situation, but instead the potentially arresting officer became a protective minister of God's divine intervention. The police officers actually pointed out and made a passage for us to the cell phone parking lot to sleep in our rental car until the airport shuttle bus came in the wee hours of the morning. One officer offered to watch over us to make sure no one would bother us until it was time to get the shuttle to the airport terminal. There were so many God-inspired episodes to retrieve my sister-in-law that a whole chapter might not be sufficient to tell of God's delivering power. We traveled with her back to Massachusetts and spent the last few months moving her first to hospital care and then into a nursing home in the Boston area. She has been treated very well by the medical staff at Massachusetts General Hospital and she is now living in community with family.[14]

Yvonnette O'Neal

In the twenty-plus years I have known Yvonnette O'Neal, she has created space for meaningful growth and change in race relations. As founder of Ambassadors Network Ministry, she fosters empathy as she builds social connections. As an African American woman, she promotes peace and reconciliation.

> As an American church leader, Yvonnette O'Neal, founder of My Child Ministry, attended the memorial celebration of the fiftieth anniversary of Dr. King's March on the Washington, DC Mall and commented favorably on the strong feeling of goodwill that prevailed among brothers and sisters of every color who attended. Ms.

14. Davis and DeFazio, *The Commission*, xii.

O'Neal explained that Dr. King was a pastor who understood that each Christian serves God by bringing souls to Jesus and that his civil rights activism sprang from his devotion to prayer and his obedience to God's word.[15]

As an African American child at the height of the civil rights movement in Mississippi, Yvonne was integrated into all-white schools. This experience taught her to relate to the individual independent of race, color, or creed. In southeast Washington, DC, as a young adult on staff at the Frederick Douglass Center and the Fishing School, her ethnic background gave her the education and social skills necessary to teach the predominately African American inner-city students how to develop in order to succeed in a multicultural society.[16]

Through overcoming the challenges of her background, Yvonne has developed the ability to reach out in a multicultural church. She has ministered to mayors and members of Congress and city councils. Yvonnette expounds God's word by organizing all-night gospel praise-a-thons at the Lincoln Memorial, prayer events of Christian leaders from across the nation at historic churches in the D.C. Metro Area, and at Wailing Women International Intercessory Prayer events in key locations in the nation's capital. Her civil rights background and the profound influence of Dr. King has influenced her latest initiative to institute Bible clubs as electives in U.S. public school systems.[17]

Gemma Wenger

Gemma Wenger's reflection on her personal experience of reverse discrimination is an excellent framework for preparing readers for constructive conversations.

---

15. Jeanne DeFazio, "We Shall Overcome." no longer available to access on the Spencers' post.

16. DeFazio and Lathrop, *Creative Ways*, 24.

17. DeFazio, "Multicultural Aspect of Egalitarian Leadership," in Spencer and Spencer, *Christian Egalitarian Leadership*, 118–19.

"Choose to Look at the Heart Rather than the Outward Appearance"

When discussing racial reconciliation, I always refer to the scripture in 1 Samuel 16:7, which says, "For the Lord sees not as man sees; for man looks on the outward appearance, but God looks on the heart." Racial reconciliation comes when we are looking upon each other with the eyes of the Lord. The Lord is not looking at a person's skin color, but rather the character and integrity of his heart. Our enemy, the devil, comes to steal, kill, and destroy (John 10:10). The devil will try to divide people by their race instead of uniting people in their faith in the Lord Jesus Christ. The Bible says that the word of God is a "discerner of the thoughts and intents of the heart" (Hebrews 4:12). We as believers need to exercise the gift that God has given us to understand, identify, and discern the motives, intentions, and workings of a person's inner man. When we judge by the outward appearance as far as race or appearance is concerned, we will miss what God is trying to say to us; we will miss that one whom God has chosen to use to bless us.

Everybody has encountered racism to some degree in their lives. My first experience came as a first-year teacher in the Black and Latino communities of South Los Angeles. The moment I was hired, the power of the Holy Spirit showed me the spirit of racism that was operating against me as a Caucasian individual. I had never experienced racism before, but God's anointing taught me the depth of this darkness, which was clearly not of him. The interesting thing was that the person who made the most racist comments toward me was the one that God ultimately used to greatly help me. My partner kindergarten teacher, who was Black, grew up in Mississippi where racism prevailed. I remember having a conversation with her regarding her feelings about it and my heart to bring reconciliation and healing. I was surprised to learn that her intention was to fully retaliate in a manner against White individuals. She had no place in her world for White people. She was no longer accepting the role of the victim but was taking a highly aggressive retaliatory stance. Her comments against me were extremely racist, but as a Christian, I ignored it. Presenting my case to the Black principal was out of the question as I also perceived her to be quite racist. She clearly favored and promoted individuals of her own race. I was used to being chosen because people saw the excellence in my work, but this was the first time I felt overlooked. For example, I presented an instructional lesson to my first-grade students for my evaluation, and the principal, instead of commending me, stated that I was "showing off." Ultimately, though, God was in control and my partner teacher encouraged me to obtain my master's degree in educational administration to become an administrator for the school district. That very one who had hurt me so greatly with her racist rhetoric at the same time encouraged me to seek promotion. God uses those very ones who have hurt you the most to help you with that one important decision that will make a lasting impression on your life.

It is important to note that in the midst of this darkness of racism that tried to destroy me, God always made a way for me and used whomever he chose. I remember I came back from vacation at this large four-track school only to find that there was an opening as a literacy coach. No teacher who was "on track" when I was "off track" desired that position. When I came back, I applied and got it. Because there was no one else who expressed an interest in that position, it fell right into my lap. I truly believe that I never would have had a chance had a staff member of a "preferred" race applied. They would have received preferential treatment. God worked a miracle for me to promote me because I pleased him. God made a way for me in the midst of the darkness. He saw my ability, and he blessed me even when no one else would!

As someone who ministers to those on skid row and in prisons as well as internationally on television and radio, I truly seek to have the heart of the Lord toward all races, nations, and cultures. I appreciate the diversity that all individuals contribute. I don't value one nationality above another. One time, I attended a professional development whereby the instructor was lecturing on racism.

Defining Strategies and Frameworks

He told everyone to say to themselves, "I am racist!" I refused and told my Latina partner that I wasn't going to say it because it wasn't true. My partner then proceeded to loudly call me a liar and stormed off. First of all, I was shocked. Her response truly caught me off guard. I was also incredibly hurt, but at the same time, I refused to have someone put something on me that was an absolute fallacy. The entire experience was an eye-opener though. It did show me that my Latina partner viewed all White people, including me, as racists. It appeared that she grouped all White people together in a big bundle and did not look at them as individuals. For someone whom I had just met, who didn't know me at all, to call me a liar really was enlightening as far as showing me how the world perceives White people. All I can do is respond in love no matter how I am judged. My role is to be that one that creates harmony and peace through the power and love of the Lord Jesus Christ in a dark and divided world. I am going to ignore the works of darkness and focus on the work that God is doing in my life and the people that he has placed there.

One time I was seeking for multiple doors to be open, and they all shut in my face. I said to myself, "If I were Black, I would think that these people were racist." What the Lord was showing me was that he shut those doors, not based on the color of my skin, but he had another direction for me. When God shuts a door, some would like to resort to saying, "They are racist," when that might not be the case at all. We need to seek God's understanding in all things and know that he truly will open the right doors.

As one who has experienced the ugliness of racism firsthand, I would never treat anyone in the manner as I have been treated. I would never wish that inequitable treatment on another; and therefore, I strive to be led by the Spirit of God and look at the heart of man rather than the outward appearance. I desire to have the mind of Christ when it comes to discerning the character of man. I know that I will prosper because my God will make a way for me even when others are slamming doors in my face. When doors are shut, it is so important to seek the door that God, by his Spirit, would open for you. Our goal is to please the Lord even in the face of opposition and injustice. Those who are willing to work hard and conduct their affairs in wisdom will succeed if they don't give up!

Unbeknownst to most people, racism can protect you on the job from the capriciousness of supervisors. Some superiors will not arbitrarily come against a person of a different race unless it is a serious issue and they have just cause and corroborated evidence, out of fear of being accused of racism. One may be at more of a disadvantage with superiors of the same race because they will feel free to criticize minute details. The fear of being called a racist can halt unfair and unjust treatment with no evidentiary merit.

In another instance, my mother and I visited a large Black church in Los Angeles. They received us with open arms and ministered to us the warmth of the love of God. There was no racism, only Christians ministering to other Christians as the Lord instructed in his word. We all came together in the "unity of the Spirit" (Ephesians 4:3) to do the work of the Lord as followers of Christ. The Holy Spirit breaks down walls of racism and creates oneness in his body whereby all members are working together toward a common goal to build the kingdom of God. Racism tears down the body of Christ, but the Spirit restores and heals. God does not judge by the color of one's skin; in fact, he created your appearance to glorify him. We as Christians need to value all of God's diverse creation just as he does.

The pain of racism is real. I know the deep wounds from promotions that were never offered to me because of my race when I was truly qualified for the job. I know the financial loss of not getting that promotion, and its profound effect on my life. At the same time, though, those who are of the same spirit will recognize the Spirit of God in you, and God will open the right door for you. Our God knows how to break through that evil spirit of racism. Don't allow racism to rule your life. Allow the forgiveness and love of the Lord to flow from you into others to minister the healing grace of the Lord. Let God control your life completely and have faith that he can touch even the most racist heart to do his will.[18]

---

18. Gemma Wenger, interview by email, February 16, 2021.

Section Two

Diversity and Inclusion in the Interracial Family

> New analysis from Pew Research indicates that the number of multiracial or multiethnic infants has tripled since 1980, making up to 14 percent of infants born in 2015. The growth coincides with the rise of interracial marriages, which has more than doubled in that time as well.[1]

THESE THOUGHTFUL STATEMENTS ON the interracial family describe an opportunity for multiple and mixed identities in the world who can deal with diversity.

Mary Ann DeFazio

What is beautiful about Mary Ann's account is the fact that in a world marked by racial division, her biracial family is evidence that races can coexist happily in the same home.

---

1. Yam, "Number of Multiracial, Multiethnic Babies," lines 3–6.

As a grandmother of a biracial granddaughter, I am contributing to this dialogue taking a stand against ethnic stereotypes.[2]

These two entrees are excerpts from my journal.

Friday, May 29: The weather has been scorching hot these past three days but is beginning to cool today. What a relief. As a happy, early start to our day, Allie and I took a long, cool walk and scooter-ride around the neighborhood. We both enjoyed it. I'm worried that what once seemed impossible now seems quite routine. When I first imagined being in quarantine for two, possibly three weeks, I could barely stand the thought. It now feels normal. Other than my walks around the neighborhood and the occasional lonely drive, It is routine. That does not mean I'm happy about it. In fact, I've struggled with sadness and loneliness. It's difficult for all of us. Poor Allie is feeling caged. It's not normal for a girl, almost six, to stay away from the kids she loves to play with. Christina keeps her engaged with activities and school-time distance learning with her teacher. We also play! We have fun. We do baking, cooking, and science projects, and make messes. But it's not the same. I feel sorry for her. Now, as Sacramento County Stay Home restrictions begin to loosen, I am not feeling any better. I predict that we will see a spike in infections and that means it's more dangerous for me to go anywhere. I want this to be over.

Monday, June 1: Last Monday, May 25, there was an act of violent restraint by a Minneapolis police officer on a man suspected of passing a counterfeit bill at a store. The man, who was held down by a knee on his neck for over eight minutes, while in handcuffs, was named George Floyd. Mr. Floyd died of apparent asphyxiation, there on the street, with three other officers watching. Since that day, now one week ago, there have been protests. Black Lives Matter! I have always believed this truth. Now, as the grandmother of a bi-racial child, it's personal. The protests were first in Minneapolis but have since spread to several other major cities and small towns all around the country.

---

2. Mary Ann DeFazio, interview by email, February 2, 2021.

Sacramento is, tonight, in the midst of its fourth night of protest, or as they now have become riots. Tonight, Sacramento has declared the city shut down, from 8:00 P.M. until 6:00 A.M. There has been growing violence and destruction and I believe there will be more tonight.

Violence isn't the answer. It dilutes and bastardizes the meaning and dignity by which BLM operates. I believe that the damage is being done by people whose message hasn't been heard. It hasn't been heard for generations! There is anger! I am angry. But violence isn't the answer! The message of Peaceful demonstration is being ignored. But violence is the wrong message. I pray that dignity will someday soon be afforded to all people of our country, especially those of us who have waited generations to be seen.[3]

Lori Chang

When Howard and I got married in the summer of 1994, it was a beautiful day. A perfect day. We both grew up in California and my mum, being from Canada, and Howard, growing up Chinese-American, didn't really give me any second thoughts with regard to race. On the contrary, I enjoyed my multicultural experience. My best friend was Korean-American and Howard's best friends were Chinese-American like him. I also had Caucasian friends. We both did. But we didn't face prejudice as a married couple until the first few years we were married. Our oldest daughter looked almost exactly like her father at birth. My mum and I walked into Costco with the baby a few months after she was born. A woman stopped us near the front entrance, looked at my daughter, and exclaimed, "Oh, you have an Asian baby! Did you adopt?" Fortunately, I moved past my reaction of feeling offended and my teacher's brain kicked in. I calmly replied, "No, this is my baby I gave birth to. I am here today shopping with my mom and my husband is Chinese-American. I

---

3. Davis and DeFazio, *Commission*, 18. Mary Ann DeFazio, interview by email, September 17, 2020.

remember her eyes got wide and she mumbled something like, "Ohh how nice!" and walked away. I feel educating people, opening them up to the option of interracial marriage is important. Their reaction is going to be their reaction, but we can try to involve others in conversation and share our unique perspectives. When my daughter turned three, we went to Canada to visit my mum's family. After we got past the questioning eyes from the border patrol at the Washington/British Columbia border (seeing my White face allowed us to drive into Canada without hesitation; coming back, a different team of border patrol decided to search our car), my younger cousins were curious about this husband of mine. Once they found out he was a hockey fan and played roller hockey, they swept him away for the rest of the afternoon. He became part of the family that day. Finding common ground through activities, whether sports, music, dining preferences, etc., can bond people from diverse ethnic backgrounds. I have witnessed it myself.[4]

Linda Lockhart

As a young woman of Cape Verdean descent, I gave birth to two wonderful daughters in a relationship with an African American man. I cherish my daughters with all my heart. The relationship was fought with difficulty. The breakup was hard on the children but my daughters did benefit from a loving relationship with their father's mother. They have strong ties to my Portuguese-American family. We are a tight-knit family and have overcome financial and health crises. I am the loving grandmother and great grandmother of multiracial children. I have deep and abiding faith in Jesus as my Rock and Redeemer. I instilled in my children and grandchildren the understanding that they are "accepted in the beloved" according to Ephesians 1:6: "To the praise of the glory of his grace, wherein he hath made us accepted in the

---

4. Lori Chang, interview by email, February 4, 2021.

beloved." I always keep open lines of communication with my children and grandchildren. We may not always agree but we speak our minds freely and openly with one another. We tell each other how we feel about everything. That is how we deal with the prejudice they often face.[5]

Conclusion

Thanks to these contributing authors whose conversations allow us to understand the experience of people who have a bias against them. This collection of conversations offers some ideas and strategies. What is the next step?

> The United States right now is a country ravaged by two sicknesses, a global pandemic, and the violence of racism. Both simultaneously demand a response and seem to swallow up anything most ordinary people are capable of doing, to render our best intentions and actions impotent in the face of these deadly plagues . . . So the question arises, when we feel paralyzed, when we feel impotent, when we feel stuck, what is God's call to us? . . . God's call is not something we plan for the future, but what we do right now in this and every moment. God's call does not cease.[6]

You can build a bridge against the racial divide by beginning your own conversations:

> Discuss your earliest memory connected to race. What did you learn from that experience? What stereotypes have you heard applied to your race or ethnicity? How does that impact you or your perspective? What are your thoughts on the state of racial justice in the U.S. today? After reading/watching/listening to a book, movie, article, or podcast about race, what stands out for you?[7]

---

5. Linda Lockhart, interview by phone, February 24, 2021.
6. Hall, "What Is God's Call?"
7. Spike, "How to Have," lines 334–52.

> One of the most basic things we all share in spite of class, race, economic status, or age is our need to eat.[8]

One of the best ways to promote racial reconciliation is sitting down at a table and sharing a meal with friends from all over the world! A strategy that I have noticed over the years to be highly successful is including diverse groups of people at a potluck meal. Dr. William David Spencer held a very popular fall semester theology course potluck meal on the Boston campus of Gordon-Cornwell Seminary. The Asian, African, Haitian, Brazilian, and African American food on the menu was a great hit! Students loved it and learned to value and appreciate their classmates' cultures. Students and faculty shared personal anecdotes from their own history and cuisine. Hosting a potluck provides food, a good time, and an opportunity to share and connect. I have photos of multicultural potluck events that I have posted on social media over the years bringing back great memories, blurring color lines, and promoting interracial harmony.

Give it a try!

---

8. Woodrum, "Longing for Nourishment," lines 17–18.

Afterword

The Church Can Lead the Way to Racial Reconciliation[1]

FRANCOIS W. AUGUSTIN

EGALITARIAN MULTIETHNIC LEADERSHIP, PARTICULARLY in America, promotes gospel expansion and sets a standard for discipleship for the global church. Jesus and the early church gave us the model for multiethnic leadership. After healing the servant of the centurion in the Gospel of Matthew, Jesus used that centurion's faith to teach the Jews how to respond to God in faith. He said, "Truly I tell you, I have not found anyone in Israel with such great faith" (Matt 8:10, 26, NIV). After Jesus healed a demon-possessed man, Mark and Luke record how that man became a traveling evangelist in the region and made quite an impact, "And he went away and began to proclaim in the Decapolis how much Jesus had done for him; and everyone was amazed" (Mark 5:20; Luke 8:39). In the story of the Samaritan woman at the well, the Gospel of John records how that woman became the leading evangelist in her town and that many came to faith in Jesus Christ through her ministry (John

1. Francois W. Augustin, interview by email, February 17, 2021.

4:39). In these three cases, we see the gospel accounts affirming the leadership expressions of non-Jewish gospel proclaimers. This was significant because the proclamation of Jesus' gospel was a task designated to the early Jewish apostles and leaders (see Matt 28:16–20). By having non-Jews partake in that task, the leadership of non-Jews was put on par with that of their Jewish counterparts. We also see in the early church leaders such as Timothy and Titus, in Timothy's case a bicultural Jew, and a non-Jew in Titus's case. To Jesus and the early church, egalitarian multiethnic leadership was the norm.

Unfortunately, the leadership experience in today's Christian church in America is very far from the realities that were known to the early church. Today, a similar antagonism to that which existed between the Jews and Gentiles in the New Testament exists in contemporary American society between Whites and non-Whites, especially with the former treating the latter as inferior groups of people. This sentiment, as it relates to the American Christian experience, is what many are now calling "White evangelicalism,"[2] or White cultural hegemony clothed with religious beliefs and practices. White evangelicalism serves as the primary hindrance to the normalization of egalitarian multiethnic leadership in America. I therefore propose a threefold approach to promote egalitarian multiethnic leadership in the United States: moving from awareness and recognition to full embrace of non-White Christian leadership, seeking the blessings of deliberate integration, submitting our pursuit of happiness to a God-centered framework.

Move from awareness and recognition to a full embrace of non-White Christian leadership. One of America's most celebrated preachers pastors in a city with a significant number of White evangelicals, and yet his congregation has very few Whites in it. He is celebrated across the board by White evangelicals in non-church contexts, but White Christians in his area are not flocking

---

2. Soong Chan Rah, in his two books *The Next Evangelicalism* and *Many Colors*, explains, in detail, what is meant by White evangelicalism. Another evangelical voice is Bryan Loritts, who, in his book *Inside Outsider*, echoes Rah and elaborates on the impact of White evangelicalism on the church and the wider culture.

to his church. This is awareness and recognition but not the full embrace of someone's call, leadership, character, and gifts. White Christians in this pastors' geographical area have done the gospel a great disservice by refusing to become members at that pastor's church despite his testimony having proven him worthy of being their pastor too.

Seek the blessings of deliberate integration. In the 1920s, Dietrich Bonhoeffer deliberately joined the membership of an African American church in Harlem. There, he learned that Christ is the liberator of his people, something that was not possible for him to learn in the White churches of his days. He took this experience to Germany, where he discipled many people on how to resist the evil threat of Nazism. There is plenty to learn from a church community where one is not a member of the dominant group. Many Black Christians in America have testified to having seen their spiritual walk enhanced after joining the membership of White-dominant churches. White Christians need to learn to trust God enough and seek similar experiences and testimonies that some of their Black counterparts have known for quite some time.

We need to *submit our pursuit of happiness to a God-centered framework.* Americans' pursuit of happiness has caused many to adopt segregationist practices, thus hindering multiethnic churches from forming. White evangelicals have bought into the wider culture's understanding of happiness by creating enclaves for themselves through purchasing homes in neighborhoods that are not welcoming to their non-White counterparts, and building institutions such as schools and churches that further promote isolation. All of this is to provide themselves with what amounts to a false sense of security. Sadly, these kinds of behavior preserve an ungodly status quo. Such a segregationist ethos has also hindered gospel expansion and the growth of healthy American churches. White Christians in America need to embrace God's offer of regeneration, and thus see happiness as a byproduct of belonging to God, as opposed to it being the output of one's material gains in American society.

Afterword

I believe if our White evangelical brothers and sisters were to deliberately attend churches led by pastors who are not White and become neighbors to people who are not White, they would set a high bar for discipleship for the entire body of Christ.

About the Authors

Francois W. Augustin is the planting pastor of The Livingstone Church—Boston (TLC), a multiethnic church that meets in the Jamaica Plain section of Boston. He was ordained at the congregation Lion of Judah in 2017 by a multiethnic panel of pastors from four different Boston-area churches. His church planting experience spans more than two decades. His multiethnic church leadership experience started at the congregation Lion of Judah, Boston's largest Hispanic church, where he served on the Spanish ministries worship team and helped launch a Saturday English service. Later, Rev. Augustin served on the planting team of a Haitian American church in Boston. After graduating from seminary, he spent two years belonging to and supporting Asian and Anglo-led churches prior to planting TLC. For the past three years, he has been leading global IT projects for a Fortune 500 corporation, primarily serving their European division. In addition to ministry practice, during his seminary years, he was a Byington research scholar who supported the initial research for *Reaching for the New Jerusalem: A Biblical and Theological Framework for the City* (Wipf & Stock, 2013). Following graduation, he served as an Athanasian teaching scholar with William David Spencer at Gordon-Conwell Theological Seminary and has been a regular contributor to the *Africanus Journal*. Rev. Augustin holds a BS with honors from UMass Amherst, where he also graduated as a member of the International Scholars Program.

Later, he earned an ALM from Harvard University and an MDiv, *magna cum laude*, from Gordon-Conwell Theological Seminary.[1]

Jeanne DeFazio is a SAG/AFTRA (Screen Actors Guild / American Federation of Television and Radio Artists) actress of Spanish-Italian descent, who played supporting parts in theater, movies, and television series, then served the marginalized in the drama of real life. She became a teacher of second language–learner children in the barrios of San Diego. She completed a BA in history at the University of California–Davis, an MAR in theology at Gordon-Conwell Theological Seminary, and the Cal State TEACH English language learners program. From 2009 to the present, she has served as an Athanasian Teaching Scholar at Gordon-Conwell's multicultural Boston Center for Urban Ministerial Education. She is the coeditor of *Creative Ways to Build Christian Community*, *Redeeming the Screens*, and *Empowering English Language Learners*, and *An Artistic Tribute to Harriet Tubman*. Jeanne is a contributing author to *Christian Egalitarian Leadership*. She coauthored with Teresa Flowers *How to Have an Attitude of Gratitude on the Night Shift* and edited *Berkeley Street Theatre*, *The Commission, Keeping the Dream Alive: A Reflection on the Art of Harriet Lorence Nesbitt*, and *Specialist Fourth Class John Joseph DeFazio: Advocating for Disabled American Veterans*.[2]

Martha Reyes was born in Puerto Rico and has resided in California, ministering to Hispanics in the United States and internationally, since 1978. She has traveled to more than twenty-two Latin American countries and many parts of Europe and the Middle East, giving concerts and retreats on inner healing and participating as a guest speaker in national and international conventions on healing and restoration. From 1992 until the year 2000 she organized the acclaimed

---

1. Spencer and Spencer, *Christian Egalitarian Leadership*, ix-x.
2. Spencer and Spencer, *Christian Egalitarian Leadership*, xi.

About the Authors

Hosanna Multi-Festivals conventions, international events with representatives from thirty countries in music, theater, and arts, held annually in Mexico, Florida, and Israel.[3]

Olga Soler is a director/writer and performer for Estuary Ministries, a Christ-centered performing arts ministry dealing with biblical themes, inner healing, abuse, and addictive problems. The art forms used include drama, dance, storytelling, mime, comedy, graphic arts, writing, film, and song. Olga attended the High School of Performing Arts ("Fame"), the Lee Strasberg Theatre and Film Institute, and the Herbert Berghof Studio in New York City. She has performed widely at conferences, churches, prisons, coffee houses, support groups, youth groups, and retreats and has even performed on the streets, at secular colleges, and in worship services across the United States and the United Kingdom. She holds degrees in education and communications with equivalent studies in theology and psychology. She studied for two years at Gordon-Conwell Theological Seminary. She has designed and conducted the workshops "Dance Alive" and "Trauma Drama" at many Christian recovery conferences. She wrote the curriculum for and conducted discovery groups for addicts at the Boston Rescue Mission, using the arts to help them process aspects of their recovery. She also conducts workshops for Christian drama and dance in many churches of all denominations. Using Paulo Freire's *Pedagogy of the Oppressed*, she wrote a script for the Mosaics group of parents, helping their children, who were victims of sexual abuse, through the court system and assisted them in filming the script for a documentary. She performed and coauthored scripts for four years with the Christian ministry named Team in Massachusetts and conducted eight full-scale multimedia presentations out of the Rio Ondo Arts Place in Woburn, Massachusetts, including *Voice of the Martyrs*, *Techno Easter*, and *Clean Comedy Night*. She has directed and choreographed entire productions at universities

---

3. DeFazio and Spencer, *Redeeming the Screens*, 90–91.

About the Authors

and colleges, including *A Man for All Seasons*, *Jane Eyre*, *Amal and the Night Visitors*, and (by permission of the author) Calvin Miller's *The Singer*. She wrote and illustrated the book *Epistle to the Magadalenes* and has conducted retreats for women using the book accompanied by dramatic presentation. She is the author of many other books and assorted screenplays. She is the proud mother of three wonderful children, Cielo, Reva, and Ransom. She lives in Massachusetts with her husband, Chris, and her Japanese Chin (dog), Kiji.[4] Email: fleursavag@yahoo.com

---

4. See DeFazio, *Keeping the Dream Alive*, 32–33.

Bibliography

Almquist, Curtis. "Making Meaning." *Cowley* 47/1 (Fall 2020) n.p. https://issuu.com/ssje/docs/2020_cowley_fall__pages.
"Arts Health and Well-Being." The Welsh NHS Confederation. May 2018. https://www.nhsconfed.org/-/media/Confederation/Files/Wales-Confed/Literature-review-of-arts-and—health-and-wellbeing.pdf.
Boud, David. "What Is Peer Learning and Why Is It Important?" Unpublished paper.
Davis, Julia C. *An Artistic Tribute to Harriet Tubman*. Edited by Jeanne C. DeFazio and Julia C. Davis. Eugene, OR: Resource, 2021.
DeFazio, Jeanne C., ed. *The Commission: The God Who Calls Us to Be a Voice during a Pandemic, Wildfires, and Racial Violence*. Eugene, OR: Wipf & Stock. 2021.
———. *Keeping the Dream Alive: A Reflection on the Art of Harriet Lorence Nesbitt*. Eugene, OR: Resource, 2019.
———. "We Shall Overcome." September 14, 2013. http://blogs.christianpost.com/scriptural-truths/we-shall-overcome-177918/.
DeFazio, Jeanne, and John P. Lathrop, eds. *Creative Ways to Build Christian Community*. Eugene, OR: Wipf & Stock, 2013.
DeFazio, Jeanne, and William David Spencer, eds. *Empowering English Language Learners*. Eugene, OR: Wipf & Stock, 2018.
———, eds. *Redeeming the Screens: Living Stories of Media "Ministers" Bringing the Message of Jesus Christ to the Entertainment Industry*. Eugene, OR: Wipf & Stock, 2016.
Flowers, Teresa, and Jeanne DeFazio. *How to Have an Attitude of Gratitude on the Night Shift*. Eugene, OR: Resource, 2014.
Frye, Jocelyn. "Racism and Sexism Combine to Shortchange Working Black Women." August 22, 2019. Unpublished paper.
Hall, Lucas. "What Is God's Call?" *Cowley* 47/1 (Fall 2020) n.p. https://issuu.com/ssje/docs/2020_cowley_fall__pages.
Helgeland, Brian. *42*. Screenplay. The Internet Movie Script Database. https://imsdb.com/scripts/42.html.

Bibliography

"I Have a Dream: Full Text March on Washington Speech." Delivered at the March on Washington, August 28, 1963. NAACP. https://www.naacp.org/i-have-a-dream-speech-full-march-on-washington/.

Laurence, Kenneth, and Terry Keleher. "Structural Racism." Paper for the Race and Public Policy Conference, 2004. https://drive.google.com/file/d/1niSBHRjR8pXJov_lWU_1-Nd8uoxoFl1o/view.

"A Prayer of St. Francis of Assisi." Wikipedia. https://en.m.wikisource.org/wiki/A_prayer_of_St._Francis_of_Assisi.

Spencer, Aida B., and William D. Spencer, eds. *Christian Egalitarian Leadership: Empowering the Whole Church according to the Scriptures*. Eugene, OR: Wipf & Stock, 2020.

Spike, Carlett. "How to Have a Respectful Conversation about Racial Justice." AARP, September 22, 2020. https://www.aarp.org/home-family/friends-family/info-2020/having-racial-justice-conversations.html.

Truitt, Janine. "Race Relations in the Workplace: The Role of Human Resources." *Advisorpedia*, December 15, 2014. https://www.advisorpedia.com/growth/race-relations-and-the-workplace-the-role-of-human-resources/.

Vinipal, Courtney. "5 Ways to Approach Racial Equity at Work." PBS, *News Hour*, June 5, 2020. https://www.pbs.org/newshour/nation/watch-live-answering-your-questions-on-race-in-the-workplace.

Vryhof, David. "The Nativity of John the Baptist." Sermon. Society of Saint John the Evangelist, June 25, 2013. https://www.ssje.org/2013/06/25/the-nativity-of-john-the-baptist-br-david-vryhof/.

Wang, Frances Kai-Hwa. "California Governor Signs Bill to Develop High School Ethnic Studies Curriculum." *NBC News*, September 14, 2016. https://www.nbcnews.com/news/amp/ncna648396.

Woodrum, Jim. "Longing for Nourishment." Sermon. Society of Saint John the Evangelist, May 14, 2017. https://www.ssje.org/2017/05/14/longing-for-nourishment-br-jim-woodrum/.

Yam, Kimberly. "Number of Multiracial, Multiethnic Babies Has Tripled in 35 Years: Report." *Huffington Post*, June 16, 2017. https://www.huffpost.com/entry/pew-research-multiracial-multiethnic-babies_n_594009bfe4b0b13f2c6e2440.

www.ingramcontent.com/pod-product-compliance
Lightning Source LLC
Chambersburg PA
CBHW061513040426
42450CB00008B/1599